A TO Z OF SEND

A Special Educational Needs Dictionary
for Parents and Professionals

Gemma Corby

Copyright © 2021 Gemma Corby

All rights reserved

No part of this book may be reproduced, or stored in a retrieval system, or transmitted in any form or by any means, electronic, mechanical, photocopying, recording, or otherwise, without express written permission of the publisher.

ISBN: 9798709656086

Cover design by: Art Painter
Library of Congress Control Number: 2018675309

This book is dedicated to all the parents/carers of young people with additional needs and the professionals who support them.

CONTENTS

Title Page	1
Copyright	2
Dedication	3
A to Z of SEND	11
A	12
B	18
C	19
D	24
E	29
F	34
G	37
H	39
I	42
J	45
K	46
L	47
M	49
N	53
O	55
P	57
Q	64

R	65
S	68
T	77
U	81
V	82
W	84
X	85
Y	86
Z	87
Useful Resources	88

ACRONYMS

ABI – Acquired Brain Injury

ACEs – Adverse Childhood Experiences

ADHD: Attention Deficit and Hyperactivity Disorder

APD – Auditory Processing Disorder

ASD - Autistic Spectrum Disorder

CAMHS – Child and Adolescent Mental Health Service

CBT – Cognitive Behavioural Therapy

CLA – Child Looked After

CoP – [SEND] Code of Practice

CP – Cerebral Palsy

DCD – Developmental Coordination Disorder

DLD – Developmental Language Disorder

DSL – Designated Safeguarding Lead

EAA – Examination Access Arrangements

EBD – Emotional Behaviour Difficulties

EHA – Early Help Assessment

EHCP – Education and Health Care Plan

EP – Educational Psychologist

FRAX – Fragile X Syndrome

FSP – Family Support Process

GDD – Global Developmental Delay

HI – Hearing Impairment

HLTA – Higher Level Teaching Assistant

IEP – Individual Education Plan

JCQ – Joint Council of Qualifications

LA – Local Authority

LAC – Looked After Child

LSA – Learning Support Assistant

MASH – Multi-Agency Safeguarding Hub

MD – Muscular Dystrophy

MLD – Moderate Learning Difficulties

MSI – Multi Sensory Impairment

NT – Neurotypical

OCD – Obsessive Compulsive Disorder

ODD – Oppositional Defiant Disorder

OT – Occupational Therapist/Therapy

PD – Physical Disability

PDA – Pathological Demand Avoidance

PEP – Personal Education Plan

PMLD – Profound and Multiple Learning Disabilities

PR – Parental Responsibility

PT – Physiotherapist or Physiotherapy

PTSD – Post Traumatic Stress Disorder

QFT – Quality First Teaching

SALT/SLT – Speech and Language Therapist/Therapy

SEMH – Social, Emotional and Mental Health

SENCO – Special Educational Needs Coordinator

SEND – Special Educational Needs and Disabilities

SLCN – Speech, Language and Communication Needs

SLD – Severe Learning Difficulties

SpLD – Specific Learning Difficulty

TA – Teaching Assistant

VI - Visual Impairment

ZPD – Zone of Proximal Development

A TO Z OF SEND

This is a practical dictionary of specialist terms and an essential tool for anyone who supports children and young people with additional needs, in any capacity.

Whether you are a parent/carer trying to navigate a minefield of jargon and acronyms, or you work with young people with special educational needs, this book will inform you of the pertinent key terms, conditions, specialists, external agencies and strategies to help you effectively support the most vulnerable young people.

This book also includes a list of useful resources. Visit www.gemmacorby.com for a hyperlinked and regularly updated version of these resources.

A

Acquired Brain Injury (ABI)

An ABI is an injury caused to the brain since birth. There are many possible causes, including traumatic brain injury (e.g., caused by a road traffic accident or a fall), tumours and strokes, to name but a few.

Students with ABI may struggle with aspects of organisation, sequencing tasks, concentration, social interactions, emotional regulation and memory. They will therefore require additional support.

Adverse Childhood Experiences (ACEs)

ACEs is the term used to describe the trauma experienced by young people before the age of 18, which can have negative lifelong emotional and physical impacts. Long-term, severe stress can alter the way in which the brain functions. Young people who have experienced trauma are more likely to present with challenging behaviours (e.g., confrontational behaviour, or withdrawn and disassociated behaviour).

Some examples of ACEs include abuse, witnessing domestic violence and exposure to substance abuse.

See Fight, Flight and Freeze, Hypervigilance and Threat Perception.

Amblyopia

Amblyopia is the medical term for a 'lazy eye'. It is a condition where the vision does not properly develop; it is estimated to affect one in fifty children.

Amblyopia occurs when one or both eyes are unable to develop a strong connection to the brain. Most commonly only one eye is impacted, with the child relying more on the 'good' eye.

Annual Review

These are review meetings for students with Education and Healthcare Plans (EHCPs), and as the name suggests they take place yearly. In secondary schools it is unlikely that class teachers will attend the review meeting, however they will be asked for their views on the young person's progress in relation to the four broad areas of need. It is a statutory requirement that all teachers supply this feedback.

The review meeting is usually attended by the young person, their parents/carers, the SENCO and other professionals; since cuts were made as part of the austerity drive, it is often the case that fewer external agencies are able to attend than in the past. The review is child-centred so usually the young person gives their views and aspirations for the future first; then their parents/carers, the school and the other professionals share their views.

At points of transition (i.e., between key stages) the annual review meeting will also be attended by a representative of the local authority (LA). This is true of academies and free schools too.

See Four Areas of Need.

Anxiety

Anxiety is a persistent feeling of unease which can range from mild to severe. It may manifest in physical symptoms such as stomach pains, loose stools and skin rashes.

It is usual for people to experience some anxiety at times (e.g., when sitting examinations) but some young people struggle to manage their anxieties, and this can impact their daily lives. Anxiety can also be a symptom of several other conditions, including ADHD, autism and learning difficulties.

See Fight, Flight or Freeze and Social Anxiety Disorder.

Aphasia

Aphasia is a significant difficulty with speaking or understanding language as a result of damage to the brain. Causes of aphasia include strokes, traumas to the head, brain tumours, brain infections or neurodegenerative diseases (e.g., dementia).

Asperger's

Asperger's Syndrome is just another name for autism. Some people have come to associate Asperger's with higher functioning autism, but this is inaccurate. The reason for the development of the two terms is historical.

In 1943, Austrian-American psychiatrist Leo Kanner published an English language paper on autism, which he labelled "infantile autism". At roughly the same time, Austrian physician Hans Asperger published his paper *Die Autistischen Psychopathen* (1944), which (as you have probably worked out) was written in German.

I am not sure if you know what was going on in the world in the first half of the 1940s, but without going into details, suffice to say that the English and the German-speaking worlds were not on the best of terms. As a result, these two ideas developed separately, although they are the same.

Asperger's is not 'mild autism', and it is important to recognise this, as neglecting to do so can have serious consequences for the young people with this diagnosis.

Assess, Plan, Do, Review

See Graduated Approach.

Attachment Conditions

Attachment conditions occur when a child has been unable to consistently connect with a parent/primary caregiver. They can also be the result of adverse childhood experiences.

A young person with attachment issues may present as very needy, constantly demanding attention; alternatively, they may be withdrawn, controlling, hostile or angry.

See Adverse Childhood Experiences.

Attention Deficit Disorder (ADD)

Attention Deficit Disorder (ADD) is no longer a medical diagnosis but is sometimes used to refer to the predominantly inattentive type of ADHD. However, the term ADHD is officially used to describe both the hyperactive and inattentive subtypes of attention deficit and hyperactivity disorder. Many people continue to use the term ADD, even though it is not a diagnosis.

Attention Deficit Hyperactivity Disorder (ADHD)

ADHD is similar to autism as it is a spectrum, neurodevelopmental condition which requires a medical diagnosis. Most cases are identified in children aged between six and twelve years old and, according to the NHS website: "People with ADHD can seem restless, may have trouble concentrating and may act on impulse."

People with ADHD may also experience additional conditions, such as sleep and anxiety disorders, dyslexia and autism. Although it is important to be clear that ADHD is not a mental health condition, many people with the condition experience mental health difficulties (in some cases as a result of not receiving a timely diagnosis).

ADHD is recognised as a lifelong disability, which can influence the future emotional wellbeing and success of young people, if the appropriate support is not offered.

The ADHD Foundation offers excellent advice, training and resources – a link to their website can be found in Useful Resources.

See Comorbid Conditions.

Atypical Autism

A person is diagnosed with atypical autism when they share the majority of characteristics of autism but not all. Similarly, they may struggle with aspects of social communication - including understanding non-verbal cues and social boundaries – as well as preferring routine and experiencing sensory processing differences. Like autism, it is a spectrum condition.

See Autism.

Auditory Processing Disorder (APD)

Auditory processing disorder is where a person has difficulty understanding sounds, including spoken words. It is a result of how the brain interprets sound; it is not a physical difficulty with the way sound is carried through the ear.

Students with APD may find it challenging to understand speech in noisy environments; people who speak quickly and/or have a strong accent; similar sounding words and spoken instructions. APD is not usually diagnosed in children under the age of seven.

See Hearing Impairment.

Autism (also known as Autistic Spectrum Disorder or ASD)

Autism is a complex, lifelong developmental disability which usually impacts a person's social skills, communication, relationships, and self-regulation. Although no two people with autism are identical, just as no two neurotypical people are the same, autism is defined by a certain set of behaviours and is a spectrum condition that impacts individuals differently and to varying degrees.

Autism, like ADHD requires a medical diagnosis, where practitioners will look for evidence of persistent social communication and social interaction challenges (e.g., taking things literally or appearing 'socially awkward'); persistent difficulties with social imagination and flexibility of thought (e.g., struggling to see something from another person's perspective); persistent repetitive and restrictive behaviours (e.g., keeping to a strict routine and disliking change), as well as sensory challenges (e.g., being over or under sensitive to touch, smell, light and/or sound). People with autism may also experience extreme anxiety and meltdowns/shutdowns.

See Neurotypical.

The National Autistic Society's website contains a wealth of useful information – go to Useful Resources.

B

Barriers to Learning

This is a broad term, encompassing a variety of difficulties which make learning more challenging for young people. They include diagnosed special educational needs (e.g., dyslexia or autism); medical difficulties (where students may be required to miss a lot of school) as well as emotional and physical challenges.

Behavioural Difficulties

Also known as Emotional Behavioural Difficulties (EMD). Some children and young people may struggle to identify and/or communicate how they are feeling – especially if they are distressed. Any form of persistent, challenging behaviour could be a young person's way of telling people that something isn't right, and they are not happy. This behaviour could present as defiance, aggression or withdrawal – to name but a few examples.

Broad Areas of Need

See Four Areas of Need.

C

Care Order

A Care Order is where the local authority (LA) is given parental responsibility (PR) of a child/children. They will share it with current PR holders (usually the child's parents), however the LA has greater power in order to safeguard the welfare of a child, as necessary.

Please note, not all children who are subject to a Care Order have additional learning needs, however the trauma of this experience may lead to social, emotional and mental health difficulties, so it is good practice for the school's SENCO to be aware or involved in some capacity.

Care Plan for CLAs

All looked after children must have a Care Plan completed and updated by their social worker. Before a Court grants a Care Order it must be satisfied that a suitable Care Plan has been put in place.

The purpose of the plan is to safeguard the child and promote their best interests. It sets out overall aims, offers timescales, and sums up the needs of the child and any services required to meet those needs. In addition, it will discuss the placement of the young person, any healthcare plans and any educational needs. It is regularly revisited at Looked After Reviews.

See Care Order.

Cerebral Palsy (CP)

Cerebral palsy is the name for a group of lifelong conditions which impact movement and coordination. It can occur if a baby's brain does not develop normally while they are in the womb, or if it is damaged during or soon after birth. The severity of symptoms varies massively; some people only experience minor difficulties, while others may be severely disabled. Therefore, children with cerebral palsy may attend mainstream or specialist schools.

It is a lifelong condition, but treatments are available to help people be as active and independent as possible. These include physiotherapy, speech and language therapy and occupational therapy (all of these are detailed in this book).

Child and Adolescent Mental Health Service (CAMHS)

CAMHS is the term for the main specialist NHS community service within the wider Children and Young People's Mental Health Services (CYPMHS).

CAMHS offers a specialist, multidisciplinary mental health service, usually consisting of psychiatrists, psychologists, social workers, nurses, mental health support workers and occupational therapists among others.

Child Looked After (CLA)

This is the more modern term for a Looked After Child (LAC).

A Child who is Looked After is in the care of the Local Authority, either through a voluntary agreement with their parents or through a Care Order. They may live with foster carers or other family members or they may reside in a Children's Home.

Please note, not all looked after children have additional learning needs, however the trauma of this experience may lead to social, emotional and mental health difficulties, so it is good practice for the school's SENCO to be aware or involved in some capacity.

Clinical Psychologist

Clinical Psychologists work with people who are experiencing behavioural, emotional and/or psychological distress which is disrupting their everyday functioning and wellbeing. They may offer cognitive behavioural therapy to reduce distress and promote wellbeing.

See Cognitive Behavioural Therapy.

Code of Practice (CoP)

See SEND Code of Practice.

Cognition and Learning

One of the four broad areas of need – as outlined in the Code of Practice.

Cognition and Learning refers to barriers to learning relating to difficulties in understanding, retention of information, retrieval of information and organisation. Specific learning difficulties (SpLD) such as dyslexia, dyspraxia and dyscalculia fall under this category, as do severe learning difficulties (SLD) and profound and multiple difficulties (PMLD).

See Four Areas of Need.

Cognitive Behavioural Therapy (CBT)

This is a talking therapy to help people manage their problems by changing the way they think and behave. According to the NHS website CBT is most commonly used to treat anxiety and depression. Unlike some other talking therapies CBT addresses current problems rather than past issues.

It is essential to work with an accredited therapist. The British Association for Behavioural and Cognitive Psychotherapies (BABCP) has a register of all accredited therapists in the UK.

Cognitive Load

Cognitive Load Theory was first outlined in the late 1980s by John Sweller, an Australian Educational Psychologist.

Cognitive load is increased when extraneous demands are placed on the learner, making the task of processing information overly complex. These demands could be distractions in the classroom or perhaps the result of an additional need such as dyslexia or ADHD. Teachers can help to reduce cognitive load by providing students with support, for example writing frames and tangible learning aids (such as counters in maths).

Communication and Interaction

One of the four broad areas of need – as outlined in the Code of Practice.

Communication and Interaction refers to children and young people who experience speech, language and communication needs (SLCN). These barriers make it difficult for them to make sense of language and/or communicate effectively and appropriately with others. People with a diagnosis of ADHD and/or autism are highly likely to have difficulties with social interaction.

See Four Areas of Need.

Comorbid Conditions

Comorbidity is when there is more than one condition or illness present in the same person at the same time. Other terms include coexisting or co-occurring conditions. For example, ADHD and dyslexia are comorbid conditions, as are ADHD and sleep disorders and autism and gastrointestinal issues.

Comprehension

This refers to a person's ability to understand what they have just read. Some young people are able to confidently decode using phonics, but they do not comprehend what they have read. This is usually a result of difficulties with working memory. People with ADHD and dyslexia, for example, struggle with their working memories, often making it hard for them to read fluently and therefore engage with a written text.

D

Decoding

This is where young people use their knowledge of letter-sound relationships to correctly pronounce written words. To do this effectively they will rapidly match up a letter or combination of letters (graphemes) to their sounds (phonemes). Those with dyslexia may struggle to do this efficiently (as a result of difficulties with their working memory), impacting their fluency and therefore their comprehension.

Designated Safeguarding Lead (DSL)

The DSL is the member of the school's leadership team (SLT) with lead responsibility for child protection issues in school - although all employees in a school have a responsibility for safeguarding the children and young people in their care.

Among their many duties, the DSL will refer cases of suspected abuse (including neglect) to the local authority's children's social care; advise staff making referrals and train staff so they understand their safeguarding responsibilities. They work with professionals from a wide range of organisations, including the police.

Developmental Language Disorder (DLD)

A person with a developmental language disorder experiences significant, persistent difficulty in understanding and/or using spoken language. DLD was previously known as Specific Language

Impairment (SLI).

The cause of DLD is unknown; it is not caused by emotional difficulties or limited exposure to language. It is also not caused by other medical conditions such as autism, hearing loss or brain injuries (although young people with these difficulties may also have a language disorder).

Children with DLD may be quieter than their peers and find it difficult to express themselves verbally; their language may be immature for their age; they may experience word-finding difficulties and have a limited vocabulary; they may not understand or remember what has been said and they may struggle with reading and writing.

Differentiation

In short, differentiation acts to level the playing field, so that all students can access the curricula they are studying. This can be achieved by setting students different levels of work, according to their ability, it can also be achieved through careful questioning in the classroom, as well as the provision of support materials such as vocabulary lists, writing frames or tangible learning aids.

Dual-Coding

Simply put, this is the combined use of visuals and words, whether spoken or written. The principle of dual coding states that our brains can process information from two channels simultaneously (i.e., the things we hear and the things we see).

Dual coding can help to relieve the burden of cognitive load – for example, when a teacher is explaining something verbally, having visual prompts helps students to follow and remember what is being taught. It can be especially helpful for young people who experience difficulties with their working memory.

See Cognitive Load Theory.

Dysarthria

Dysarthria is a difficulty with the physical act of speaking as a result of brain damage or brain changes in later life (e.g., with the onset of dementia). For example, people with dysarthria may have speech that sounds slurred, difficulties with tongue and lip movements or a strained or hoarse voice, and as a result may be difficult to understand.

Dysarthria does not impact intelligence or understanding, although a person with this condition may have difficulties in these areas as well.

Dyscalculia

Dyscalculia is a persistent, specific learning difficulty (SpLD) in understanding numbers. It is distinct from other issues with mathematics in its severity of difficulties with number sense, including subitising (the ability to instantly identify the number of objects in a small group, without the need to count them), symbolic (digits) and non-symbolic (e.g., dots) magnitude comparison (i.e., the ability to identify which is the higher number or which group has the most/least dots) and ordering. It can occur by itself, but it often co-exists with other SpLDs such as dyslexia.

Dysgraphia

This is a specific learning difficulty (SpLD) where a person's writing skills are below the expected standard given their age and ability. Dysgraphia is a writing disorder associated with impaired handwriting, orthographic coding (the storing process of written words in the working memory) and finger sequencing (the movement of muscles required to write). It often co-exists with other learning difficulties such as dyspraxia and dyslexia. It does not affect all fine-motor skills.

Dyslexia

Dyslexia is a Specific Learning Difficulty (SpLD) that impacts the skills involved in accurate and fluent word reading and spelling. It occurs across the range of intellectual abilities and is best thought of as a spectrum condition. Comorbid conditions can include, speech and language difficulties, motor coordination, mental calculation, concentration and organisation.

A diagnosis of dyslexia can only be given by someone qualified to do so (e.g., an Educational Psychologist or a teacher holding the British Dyslexia Association Level Seven Diploma in Dyslexia Assessment and Intervention).

Dyslexia screeners can be carried out by anyone, regardless of their qualifications. These provide an indication as to whether a young person may or may not be dyslexic, but they are not the same as a diagnosis.

A significant report on dyslexia, from Sir Jim Rose, was published in 2009, titled: Identifying and Teaching Children and Young People with Dyslexia and Literacy Difficulties. It is more commonly referred to as the Rose Report. Read it, if you wish to learn more – see Useful Resources for the link (under Rose Report).

Dyslexia Friendly Fonts

There is little evidence to support the notion of dyslexia friendly fonts (such as Arial, Comic Sans and Sassoon), although it is acknowledged that certain fonts, such as italic typefaces slow everyone down, including people with dyslexia. In an article for the Tes, Professor John Stein, from the University of Oxford explained that letter shape is less important than between-letter and between-word spacing. In short, using larger letters and wider letter and word spacing is the best way to support dyslexic learners.

See Useful Resources for a link to this Tes article.

Dysphagia

Dysphagia is a medical term for difficulties swallowing. Dysphagia can cause individuals to cough or choke when eating or drinking, it can also result in them persistently drooling and struggling to chew food.

Dysphagia can be a result of neurological causes, due to damage to the nervous system (in the brain and spinal cord) or congenital reasons, i.e., conditions that someone is born with such as cerebral palsy, a cleft lip and palate or learning disabilities.

Dyspraxia

Dyspraxia affects a person's movement and coordination (e.g., when playing sports); it can also impact fine motor skills, such as writing or using small objects. It is a Specific Learning Difficulty (SpLD).

Dyspraxia is used interchangeably with the term Developmental Coordination Disorder (DCD).

See Fine Motor Skills and Gross Motor Skills.

E

Early Help Assessment (EHA)

The EHA has replaced the Common Assessment Framework (CAF) and is based on similar principles. The EHA is an initial assessment and planning tool that facilitates and coordinates any necessary multi-agency support. The EHA assesses the situation of the young person and their family and identifies any needs. They are most suitable for young people or families with low-level needs that can be met through short-term intervention.

Echolalia

Echolalia is a condition which causes a person to repeat previously heard words or phrases. The repetition happens apparently at random, sometimes it is immediate and at other times it is delayed. Echolalia often co-occurs with autism.

Education and Health Care Plan (EHCP)

An EHCP is for children and young people who need more support than is available through regular SEN Support (i.e., they may require regular TA support or specialist provision). It offers statutory protection for individuals aged from 0-25 years old, as long as they are in education (excluding higher education).

There are four key areas of need. A young person may have multiple needs, but their primary additional need will be stated in their EHCP. For example, a young person with a diagnosis of autism would have a primary need of Communication and Interaction, however, if they also experience anxiety and have sensory needs, it will be acknowledged in the categories Social, Emotional and Mental Health Difficulties and Sensory and/or Physical Needs respectively.

On your school management information system, students with an EHCP will be identified by the letter E, whereas those with SEND Support will have the letter K.

See Four Areas of Need.

Educational Psychologist (EP)

Schools usually buy in EP time from the local authority (although some schools may go through a private practitioner, depending on the school and the local authority). EPs support children and young people who experience learning difficulties and/or social, emotional issues. They also carry out assessments and suggest support strategies and interventions. As part of any assessment process, they will meet with parent/carers. EPs offer training and advice for school staff too.

Emotional Behavioural Difficulties (EBD)

See Behavioural Difficulties.

Emotional Literacy

Emotional literacy refers to a person's ability to communicate their emotions through words and to recognise emotions in others. To be emotionally literate, a person needs to be able to identify, manage and control their emotions. They also need to demonstrate empathy and be able to develop and maintain positive relationships with others.

Engagement Model

The engagement model has replaced P-Levels as a way of assessing learners working below the standard of national curriculum assessments, and who are not engaged in subject-specific study at key stages one and two.

The model has five areas: exploration, realisation, anticipation, persistence and initiation. Its aim is to enable schools to reflect on the progress of all their learners, in relation to the bespoke curriculum they offer them.

Assessment is based on regular observations by someone who knows the learner well. Progress through the five areas of engagement will differ for each student, according to their profile of needs, as set out in their Education and Health Care Plan. It is to be used as part of the graduated approach, measuring students' progress over time.

The model can be deployed across all key stages, including for learners attending secondary school and post-16 settings. There is no requirement for data to be submitted to the Department for Education.

Equality Act (2010)

The Equality Act legally protects people in the workplace and wider society from discrimination. It is against the law to discriminate against someone because of their age, disability, race, religion and sex, among other reasons.

This legislation is particularly relevant to young people with special educational needs (including dyslexia, autism and ADHD) as they are protected by the Equality Act. Schools have a duty to provide reasonable adjustments, so that all young people can fairly access an education that is appropriate to their needs.

The Reasonable Adjustments for Disabled Pupils Guidance [2015] by the Equality and Human Rights Commission explains this in greater depth.

See Useful Resources for the link.

Examination Access Arrangements (EAA)

These are any additional arrangements that are put in place for individuals regarding their examinations and assessments. The majority (if not all) of the students who receive EAA will be on the SEND register.

Common access arrangements include additional time (usually 25%, but it can be 50% or 100% in exceptional circumstances); a reader, a scribe, a prompt, different colour paper/colour overlays; a word processor and/or rest breaks. This is not an exhaustive list.

Schools either have someone on the staff who is specially qualified to assess students – this could be the SENCO or a higher-level teaching assistant – or the school may have an arrangement with the local authority or a particular individual or organisation.

Not all arrangements require assessment, and not all students will need to be assessed, e.g., those with a diagnosis of autism or ADHD who are seeking 25% additional time.

Evidence will need to be supplied by teachers, in a timely fashion, to show that the requested arrangements reflect the young person's "normal way of working" (this is the key phrase when it comes to EAA!).

Usually, students are assessed for EAA at the end of Year 9 – any arrangements last 26 months. Students are normally required to be reassessed when they change educational setting e.g., leaving school to attend college. The cut off point for applying for EAA is traditionally the February of the year in which the student intends to sit their examinations.

See Joint Council of Qualifications (JCQ) and Standardised Scores.

Expressive Language

Expressive language is the use of gestures, words and sentences (whether spoken or written) to convey meaning and messages to others. Key skills include being able to correctly label objects in the environment, construct grammatically correct sentences, sequence and retell stories, answer questions and describe actions and events.

Young people with expressive language difficulties can become frustrated when they are trying to express their thoughts, feelings and needs to others – potentially leading to social interaction difficulties or avoidance of social situations.

F

Family Support Process (FSP)

The Family Support Process is a shared assessment and planning framework for professionals working with children and their families. Its purpose is to assist with the early identification of needs and to promote a coordinated, multi-agency response to meet them.

The FSP can be used to support those aged between 0-19 years, including unborn children, although it can be used up to the age of 25, where a person has a learning difficulty or disability. It can be used by any organisation or practitioner who works with young people and their families and where there is a need for Early Help provision.

See Early Help Assessment.

Fight, Flight or Freeze

This is a subconscious, stress response to danger (whether real or perceived), which our ancestors evolved as part of their survival instinct. It instantly causes hormonal and physiological changes, e.g., your heart races (to increase oxygen flow to major muscles) and adrenaline surges.

Young people who experience elevated levels of stress (perhaps as a result of underlying anxiety or adverse childhood experiences), may have this response triggered more easily and frequently than their peers. For example, they may challenge staff or other students, or they may withdraw.

See Anxiety and Adverse Childhood Experiences

Fine Motor Skills

Fine motor skills are the ability to use the small muscles in the hands and wrists to make small movements e.g., writing, drawing or using scissors. Although fine motor skills come naturally to most people, they are complex and require the coordinated efforts of the brain and muscles.

Children who struggle with fine motor skills do so for a number of reasons. It could be due to a physical disability, such as cerebral palsy or or as result of a specific learning difficulty such as dyspraxia or dysgraphia.

See Dyspraxia and Dysgraphia.

Flesch-Kincaid Grade Level

See Readability.

Flesch Reading Ease Score

See Readability.

Foetal Alcohol Syndrome

If a mother drinks alcohol during pregnancy it can result in her baby having lifelong mental and physical problems; this is called foetal alcohol syndrome.

Symptoms include, a smaller than average head, short stature, distinctive facial features, learning difficulties, problems with motor control and balance, attention difficulties, health problems and issues with hearing and vision.

Four Areas of Need

The SEND Code of Practice identifies four broad areas of need in Chapter Six (sections 6.28 – 6.35). These are detailed individually in this book and are:

Cognition and Learning

Communication and Interaction

Sensory and/or Physical Needs

Social, Emotional and Mental Health Difficulties

See SEND Code of Practice.

Fragile X Syndrome

Under letter 'X'.

G

Global Developmental Delay (GDD)

The term global developmental delay is used when a child takes longer to reach particular developmental milestones, compared to their same-age peers. These include learning to walk or talk, learning new information, social interaction and motor skills.

There is some debate over the use of the term GDD by professionals, as it suggests a short-term delay that can be overcome with additional support and/or therapy; however, confusingly it can be attributed to those with a life-long disability as well.

Glue Ear

Glue ear is where the middle part of the ear canal fills with fluid, potentially causing temporary hearing loss. It can affect both ears simultaneously and is more common in children than adults.

It is important to note that when a child is experiencing glue ear, they may not be able to fully hear spoken language clearly enough to distinguish the separate sounds which make up words. This can result in the child experiencing difficulties with literacy and their speech and language skills.

Graduated Approach

The graduated approach is also known as the assess, plan, do, review cycle. It is outlined in Chapter Six (sections 6.44 – 6.56) of the SEND Code of Practice.

Students who continue to experience challenges with their learning, despite receiving quality first teaching, may require additional and/or different provision in order to meet their needs.

When accessing SEND support, students are guided through the four-part cycle of assess, plan, do, review. This allows professionals to assess the needs of an individual and refine their provision through a review process.

See SEND Code of Practice.

Graphemes

A grapheme is a written symbol, representing a sound (phoneme). It can be a single letter or a sequence of letters, e.g., sh, ch or tch.

Gross Motor Skills

Gross motor skills enable people to use the large muscles in the body, arms and legs to make whole-body movements. These skills require the coordination of the muscles and the neurological system; they impact balance, proprioception and coordination, as well as forming the basis for fine motor skills.

Children who struggle with their gross motor skills may find participating in sports challenging, this can have an impact on their informal social interactions and therefore their self-esteem.

H

Hearing Impairment (HI)

A hearing impairment is a physical difficulty with the way sound is carried through the ear and into the brain. It can be permanent or fluctuating and will substantially impact a young person's day to day life and educational performance. It is not the same as an auditory processing disorder which is the way in which the brain interprets a sound.

See Glue Ear and Auditory Processing Disorder.

Hidden Disabilities

Hidden disabilities do not have physical signs, so may not be immediately obvious. They include developmental disabilities (such as autism and ADHD), learning difficulties (such as dyslexia), mental health issues, speech and language difficulties and visual and hearing impairments. They can also include chronic illnesses such as Crohn's disease, asthma and diabetes.

Higher Level Teaching Assistants (HLTAs)

HLTAs have greater responsibility, compared to a regular TA. They may take classes on their own, run interventions and/or be in charge of Examination Access Arrangements (EAA).

Most HLTAs will have the HLTA qualification, where they will have demonstrated that they meet the required professional standards. They may also have a specialism, such as EAA, literacy or supporting young people with Social, Emotional and Mental Health (SEMH) difficulties.

See Examination Access Arrangements.

Hydrocephalus

Hydrocephalus is the build up of cerebrospinal fluid in the brain. Excess fluid can cause pressure to be exerted on the brain, which can cause damage.

Hydrocephalus can be present from birth or can occur as a result of a serious head injury or brain tumour.

Many babies born with hydrocephalus (congenital hydrocephalus) have permanent brain damage. This means that they may also have learning disabilities, issues with speech, memory difficulties, problems with coordination and possibly epilepsy.

Many children with hydrocephalus are treated using a shunt (thin tube) which is surgically implanted in the brain to drain excess fluid.

Hyperlexia

Hyperlexia is when a child can read at levels exceeding those expected for their age; they will probably be able to decode or sound out words quickly, but not necessarily comprehend what they are reading. They may have communication or speaking skills that are below the expected level for their age. There is a strong connection between hyperlexia and autism.

Hypervigilance

Hypervigilance is an increased state of alertness, where individuals are very sensitive to their surroundings. It is linked to the fight, flight or freeze response, where a person is alert to dangers, whether real or perceived.

Hypervigilance can be symptomatic of post-traumatic stress disorder, anxiety or attachment conditions and can have a negative impact on an individual's day to day life. A hypervigilant student, for example, may experience panic attacks or emotional outbursts.

See Adverse Childhood Experiences and Threat Perception.

I

Inclusive Classroom

An inclusive classroom is one which creates a supportive learning environment for all students, including those with additional needs. It is at the heart of Quality First Teaching (QFT).

An inclusive classroom takes into account the environment (e.g., are the walls too distracting for young people with ADHD? Are there any distracting noises, that might upset students with sensory needs?); the positioning of young people within the classroom (some require being nearer to the front/back of the room – depending on their needs); the different ways in which students access the curriculum (e.g., some students will require information to be presented visually, as well as spoken, they may also require different colour backgrounds/paper); how information/instructions are communicated (some will require information to be rephrased and repeated or vocabulary to be explicitly taught); how individuals learn best (do they require writing frames or tangible learning aids?) as well as consideration of any other specialist equipment (such as writing slopes and ergonomic pens).

Individual Education Plan (IEP)

These are a way for SENCOs to distil and communicate key information about a student with additional needs. They sometimes go by other names, such as pupil passports, individual learning plans or pupil profiles.

The SENCO will read an individual's professional reports and will use them to create a one-page profile to guide teachers and TAs on the best ways to support that particular student. Usually, an IEP will outline the young person's key need, will detail any relevant background information and will offer support strategies. They will also note which professional reports have been referred to, in case a teacher or TA wishes to do some more in-depth reading.

Interventions

An intervention is a way of supporting a young person with additional needs by providing them with additional help. Some local authorities refer to different "waves of intervention".

Wave One is the expectation of Quality First Teaching. This is where a teacher, and possibly a TA, has read a child's individual education plan and has put in support within the classroom. This support may include writing frames, access to a TA, provision of colour overlays and an adaptation in teaching style.

Wave Two is more targeted support, which could take the form of small group teaching, therapies or one to one support. These interventions will be timely and targeted. There will usually be a requirement for before and after data, so that the impact of the intervention can be measured.

Wave Three is where an external specialist may be asked to assess, advise or work with an individual who is not making the expected progress, despite the provisions being made by the school. For example, an educational psychologist or a speech and language therapist may be called upon to offer their specialist insights and recommendations.

Intervention offered in school can include support with literacy and numeracy; speech and language therapy; social communication and interaction groups as well as one to one mentoring.

Interventions will vary from setting to setting, depending on the needs of the students and the structure of the school/college.

See Individual Education Plan.

Irlen Syndrome

See Meares-Irlen Syndrome.

J

Joint Council of Qualifications (JCQ)

The JCQ is a membership organisation, which includes the eight largest providers of qualifications in the UK among its members.

They provide common administrative arrangements for examinations, such as access arrangements (EAA). Schools need to apply via the JCQ in order to secure EAA for their students – these may include additional time, access to a reader and/or a scribe. Each year the JCQ publishes its Access Arrangements and Reasonable Adjustments booklet (this is available as a PDF on their website). It is the definitive guide on EAA and should be referred to regularly – see Useful Resources for the link.

See Examination Access Arrangements and Standardised Scores.

K

Kinaesthetic Learning

The notion that individuals have different "learning styles" (also known as VAK – Visual, Auditory or Kinaesthetic), has largely been debunked, however, many students will benefit from a kinaesthetic approach to learning, particularly if they are struggling with certain aspects, e.g., their literacy or numeracy skills.

Kinaesthetic learning is a hands-on experience, where students learn through multi-sensory activities. This approach can be particularly useful for some dyslexic learners.

L

Learned Helplessness

Learned helplessness can occur when a student cannot see the progress that they are making. They may feel that whatever they do, or however hard they work, they will fail. This is why it is important for students to be able to see how they are progressing and have their achievements, however big or small, recognised.

Learned helplessness can also occur when adults over-support a young person, for example, constantly correcting them or giving them the right answers, and not allowing them to experience failure. This can sometimes happen when a student has one to one support.

Learning Support Assistant (LSA)

This is an alternative name for a Teaching Assistant (TA).

See Teaching Assistant.

Local Offer

Every local authority (LA) is required to write a local offer and make it available for all to access (usually via their website). A local offer is designed to give children/young people with special educational needs and their parents/carers information on the support services available in their local area.

The local offer should also include information on the available transport services and whether or not there is any financial help in order to access these services.

A link to the LA's local offer should be included on the school's SEND Information Report.

See SEND Information Report.

Looked After Child (LAC)

See Child who is Looked After.

M

Meares-Irlen Syndrome

Meares-Irlen Syndrome (also known as Irlen Syndrome or visual stress) is a perceptual difficulty which impacts the way in which the brain processes visual information, as it is unable to process full spectral light.

For those experiencing Meares-Irlen Syndrome, it can result in a range of distortions in the environment and on the printed page (students may complain of words moving or swimming on the page), as well as physical (e.g., headaches) and behavioural symptoms.

The condition can be exacerbated by factors such as artificial lighting, glare, high contrast, patterns and colours.

People with Meares-Irlen syndrome usually use coloured overlays (the colour they use will be specific to them) or glasses with coloured lenses when reading text. Schools can no longer assess for visual stress; people have to be assessed by an orthoptist. Unfortunately, colorimetry tests, where the most effective colour for overlays/lenses is determined, is not available on the NHS.

Meares-Irlen can affect people of all ages. It also appears to commonly coexist with other conditions including dyslexia, ADHD and autism.

Melatonin

Melatonin is a naturally occurring hormone that helps to control sleep patterns. Children can be prescribed a synthetic (manufactured) version if they are experiencing sleep difficulties.

Mind Mapping

This is a technique whereby learners can brainstorm their thoughts, without being concerned about order and structure. It is a useful technique in showing the connections between different ideas and concepts – thus giving students 'the bigger picture'.

Mind maps appeal to many students, particularly those who may struggle with getting something on the page (sometimes young people with additional needs can feel overwhelmed by an extended writing task), they can also be a useful revision tool. Students can organise/categorise information by employing a colour-code and they can also dual-code their mind map.

See Dual Coding.

Moderate Learning Difficulties (MLD)

Children with MLD learn at a slower pace than their peers, even with appropriate differentiated work. They will usually attain well below expected levels in all or most areas of the curriculum, despite relevant interventions. They will experience greater difficulties in acquiring basic literacy and numeracy skills; they may also have speech, language and communication needs, as well as difficulties in sustaining their concentration.

MLD is not a diagnosis and a young person with MLD may have

other learning barriers, such as dyslexia, developmental language disorder or autism. As Cowne et al state in their informative book (see Useful Resources) "Moderate Learning Difficulties is an imprecise category definition, as many children in this group will have other disabilities."

Multi-Agency Safeguarding Hub (MASH)

Multi-agency safeguarding hubs are designed to facilitate information sharing and decision making between professionals from different organisations, such as the local authority, police, schools and health agencies. They were established to improve communication and safeguard vulnerable people more effectively.

Each local authority has a MASH team, and they will be the first point of contact for safeguarding referrals to help protect the most vulnerable from harm, neglect and abuse.

Most MASH teams work to safeguard children, although some safeguard both children and adults. Your school's Designated Safeguarding Lead (DSL) will work closely with the MASH team for your local authority.

See Designated Safeguarding Lead.

Multi-Sensory Impairment (MSI)

A person with a MSI has impairments with both sight and hearing. A small number of children and young people with MSI are totally blind and deaf (deafblind), but most will have some vision and hearing. There is a huge variability in people with MSI and they may also experience other medical conditions or disabilities.

Other terms to describe MSI are dual-sensory impaired and dual sensory loss.

Muscular Dystrophy (MD)

There are several types of muscular dystrophy. They all cause progressive muscle weakness, but the areas affected, and the severity vary. Some young people with MD will need to use a wheelchair.

The NHS website details all the different types of muscular dystrophy, including Duchenne MD and Becker MD.

See Useful Resources for a link to the NHS website.

Mutism

See Selective Mutism.

N

NASEN

The National Association for Special Educational Needs (NASEN) provides advice, training and support to educational professionals.

NASENCo Qualification

All SENCOs are required to obtain the National Special Educational Needs Coordinator qualification. They have three years to do this, from when they are appointed.

Neurodevelopmental Condition/Disorder

Neurodevelopmental conditions are a group of conditions that are thought to be the result of the central nervous system not working as it should. Young people with a neurodevelopmental condition may struggle with emotional regulation, learning and self-control.

Recognised neurodevelopmental conditions include ADHD, autism, developmental language disorder, specific learning difficulties, genetic disorders (such as Fragile X Syndrome), Tourette's Syndrome, traumatic brain injuries (including those which cause cerebral palsy) and sensory processing difficulties – among others.

Neurodiversity

Neurodiversity encompasses a range of neurological differences, including ADHD, autism, specific learning difficulties (e.g., dyslexia) and developmental language disorder.

The term is thought to have been coined by activist Judy Singer in the 1990s in a bid to move away from the medical view of autism and the idea that it should be 'cured'.

American journalist, Harvey Blume, writing in 1998 for The Atlantic (see link in Useful Resources) commented: "Neurodiversity may be every bit as crucial for the human race as biodiversity is for life in general. Who can say what form of wiring will prove best at any given moment?".

Neurotypical (NT)

Neurotypical (or neurologically typical) refers to a person who does not have a diagnosis of autism.

O

Obsessive Compulsive Disorder (OCD)

OCD is where a person has obsessive thoughts and compulsive behaviours. It can affect both adults and children, with symptoms usually appearing during early adulthood (although some experience symptoms early, more often than not around puberty).

An obsession is an unwanted and unpleasant thought or urge that repeatedly enters the mind causing anxiety or disgust (e.g., a fear of one's house burning down).

A compulsion is a repetitive behaviour or mental act that you feel you need to do to temporarily relieve the unpleasant feelings brought on by the obsessive thought (e.g., repeatedly checking that appliances are switched off before leaving the house).

While it is not clear what causes OCD, it is thought a number of factors contribute, such as: unusually high brain activity or low levels of serotonin; family history; traumatic or significant life events (e.g., experiencing abuse/neglect or going through childbirth or a bereavement) and high levels of anxiety.

The main treatments are psychological therapy (often Cognitive Behavioural Therapy) and/or medication – usually a type of antidepressant to adjust the balance of chemicals in the brain is prescribed.

See Cognitive Behavioural Therapy.

Occupational Therapist/Therapy (OT)

Occupational Therapists work with people of all ages and will consider all aspects of daily life, whether at home, school or in the workplace.

Occupational therapy helps people who are physically disabled; recovering from an illness; have learning disabilities; experiencing mental health problems; have communication difficulties and/or have sensory issues.

They aim to help people live as independently as possible. They achieve this by identifying and overcoming barriers to independence. In a school context, they may support a young person who struggles to make their handwriting legible, for example.

Oppositional Defiant Disorder (ODD)

It is typical for a child/young person to be oppositional at times, however if oppositional behaviours are severe and persistent then an assessment for ODD could be appropriate.

Signs of ODD include being unusually angry; being easily annoyed; arguing with authority figures; refusing to follow rules; blaming others for mistakes and being vindictive.

P

Parental Responsibility (PR)

Parental Responsibility is defined in s 3(1) Children Act 1989 as being: "...all the rights, duties, powers, responsibilities and authority which by law a parent of a child has in relation to the child and his property".

Mothers automatically have parental responsibility, as do most fathers (unless they are not married to/in a civil partnership with the mother and/or are not named on the birth certificate).

When a child is made the subject of a care order, the local authority has legal responsibility for the child although parents continue to have parental responsibility. The local authority can limit parents' PR if it is deemed necessary in the interest of a child's welfare.

Pathological Demand Avoidance (PDA)

PDA is understood to be a profile on the autistic spectrum, describing those whose main characteristic is to avoid everyday demands and expectations.

Key features of PDA include a need for control; the avoidance of everyday demands (e.g., getting up, dressed and washed) and expectations (including things they may want and enjoy); a tendency to not respond to conventional parenting, teaching or support approaches; the use of social strategies as part of the avoidance (i.e., not just saying "no" but making excuses, withdrawing into fantasy, procrastination etc); difficulties with emotional regulation; adopting other personas (person or animal) for a prolonged period of time as well as focusing intently on one person (whether real or fictional).

Personal Budget

A personal budget can be allocated to a child's parents/carers or directly to a young person (over 16 years old) in order to secure provision as specified within the child's/young person's Education and Health Care Plan (EHCP).

A direct payment can be made, providing the parents of the child or the young person themselves accepts that various conditions are met. The local authority will state the conditions on how the personal budget should be used.

Personal Education Plan (PEP)

All looked after children must have a Personal Education Plan (PEP) as part of their Care Plan. This is a record of how professionals will support an individual's educational outcomes and achievements. It is reviewed termly by a designated teacher, the young person, their social worker and carer; the SENCO will also be in attendance, if the young person has any additional needs.

See Child Looked After and Care Plan.

Phonemes

A phoneme is the smallest unit of sound. Phonemic awareness is not the same as phonics as it involves hearing and manipulating the individual speech sounds in words, rather than writing them – remember phonemic awareness can be done in the dark! Examples of phonemes include 'a', 't', 'ch', 'sh' and 'air'.

Phonics

Phonics (also referred to as synthetic phonics) is a way of teaching reading. Children are taught two key things: that sounds are represented by written letters (graphemes) and sounds can be blended together to make words. For example, they will be taught that the letter 'm' sounds like 'mmmm'. They will then start to blend sounds together to create words (e.g., m-a-t to spell mat), this is referred to as synthesising.

Phonological Awareness

Phonological awareness is an understanding of the sound structure of a language and the ability to manipulate this structure via a range of tasks, such as separating a word into the sounds that make it up; blending single sounds into words; identifying syllables and rhyming.

Phonological Processing

Phonological processing is the use of sounds to process spoken and written language, it includes phonological awareness, phonological working memory and phonological retrieval. All three of these components are essential for the development of spoken and written language. Individuals who experience a weakness in one or more of these areas are more likely to experience literacy issues; in fact, difficulties with phonological processing are one of the key indicators of dyslexia.

Phonological Retrieval

This is the ability to recall phonemes (smallest unit of sound) associated with graphemes (written symbol representing a sound) – it is integral to phonological awareness. It is usually assessed by rapid naming tasks, for example the rapid naming of letters and numbers, whereby the individual being assessed will read out the letters or numbers presented on a chart in front of them.

Phonological Working Memory

This involves storing phoneme (smallest unit of sound) information in a temporary working memory store. This information is then available for manipulation during phonological awareness tasks, such as nonword repetition (i.e., where an assessor says a nonsense word and the learner repeats it).

See Working Memory.

Physical Disability (PD)

A physical disability is a long-term and substantial condition affecting a person's body, impairing and restricting their physical functioning, mobility, stamina and/or dexterity.

A person may be born with a physical disability or acquire it due to an accident, injury or illness.

Examples of physical disability include cerebral palsy, muscular dystrophy, epilepsy, amputations and spina bifida.

Physiotherapist or Physiotherapy (PT)

Physiotherapy is treatment to restore, maintain and/or make the most of an individual's mobility and function should they be affected by injury, illness or disability.

Physiotherapists consider the body as a whole and they can offer advice (e.g., on posture); tailor exercises to strengthen specific parts of the body and improve mobility; use their hands to help relieve pain and stiffness and encourage better movement.

Young people with physical disabilities often receive physiotherapy, sometimes this can take place in school. A physiotherapist may also attend a student's EHCP annual review, if appropriate.

Post-traumatic Stress Disorder (PTSD)

PTSD is an anxiety disorder caused by very stressful, frightening or distressing events. A person with PTSD may relive the traumatic event through flashbacks and may experience feelings of guilt, isolation and irritability. They may also have nightmares and/or have problems sleeping. Symptoms are severe and have a significant impact on everyday life.

People who repeatedly experience traumatic situations may be diagnosed with complex PTSD, it is often more severe if the trauma was experienced early in life, as it can affect an individual's development.

Symptoms of complex PTSD include feelings of shame or guilt; difficulties with emotional regulation; relationship difficulties; destructive or risky behaviour (such as self-harm) and suicidal thoughts.

Pragmatic Language

Pragmatic language skills are essential for successful social interactions – they include understanding body language (e.g., gestures or facial expressions); turn-taking in conversations; speaking at the appropriate volume and speed as well as being able to repair a conversation when it goes wrong.

Young people with autism often struggle with their pragmatic language skills, however someone who doesn't meet the full criteria for an autism diagnosis may be diagnosed with pragmatic language impairment (PLI), should they struggle with the social aspect of communication.

Processing Speed

This is the pace at which a person absorbs new information, makes sense of it and responds. Information can be auditory (i.e., spoken) or visual (i.e., words that have been written down). Processing speed is not a measure of intelligence.

Profound and Multiple Learning Disabilities (PMLD)

PMLD is when a person has a severe learning disability and other disabilities that significantly affect their ability to communicate and be independent. They may also have complex health and social care needs and require a carer or carers to support them with most areas of everyday life. Students with PMLD usually attend specialist provision rather than mainstream schools.

Proprioception

Proprioception, also known as kinaesthesia, is our sense of body awareness. Messages from muscles, joints and tendons tell us where our body is in space, including its direction, speed and force. It is this sense which allows us to safely move, without having to observe each individual motion.

Individuals who experience difficulties with this sense may exhibit balance issues, uncoordinated movements, poor posture and clumsiness.

Multiple sclerosis (MS), autism and acquired brain injuries, among other conditions, can impact the proprioception sense.

Provision Map

Provision maps show which students are in receipt of intervention that is above and beyond quality first teaching (i.e., wave one – see Interventions). They will also give the dates and frequency of any provision. They are a useful way of tracking what support an individual has received, as well as providing a bigger, whole-school picture.

There are expensive provision mapping computer programs which schools can invest in, but these are not entirely necessary. It is possible to keep you own records via Excel and whichever school management information system you use.

Pupil Passport

See Individual Education Plan (IEP).

Q

Quality First Teaching (QFT)

This term developed from a Department for Children, Schools and Families policy document in 2008. It discussed the importance of student-teacher relationships and encouraged high expectations for all learners.

The SEND Code of Practice recognises high quality teaching as being differentiated and personalised and states that special educational provision is underpinned by QFT.

Key characteristics of QFT are, well-planned lessons; high levels of teacher-student engagement and regular encouragement to engage and motivate learners.

R

Readability

This is a measure of how easy or difficult a piece of text is to read. A readability formula can be used to predict the reading level of a piece of text, based on calculations involving sentence length and the number of syllables. Readability can be expressed as an age.

Teachers and TAs can check the readability of Word documents by ensuring that the 'show readability statistics' box is checked within the review spelling and grammar section. Once a spell-check is completed a dialogue box will appear giving readability statistics. These are presented using the Flesch Reading Ease Score and the Flesch-Kincaid Grade Level.

If you do an internet search for Flesch Reading Ease and/or Flesch-Kincaid Grade Level you can find out how these correspond to different year groups (they are given using the American system but if you add one to the 'grade' you will get the English equivalent 'year' e.g., 6th Grade in the USA is Year 7 in the UK). The scores given are between 0-100, and the higher the score, the easier it is to read.

Reasonable Adjustments

Under the Equality Act (2010), all schools have a duty to make 'reasonable adjustments' to ensure that disabled students are not discriminated against. These could include the provision of a teaching assistant or specialist equipment.

The term 'reasonable' is not explicitly defined in the Equality Act, leaving it up to the discretion of the school and/or local authority to determine what is or isn't reasonable.

Receptive Language

Receptive Language is the ability to understand spoken language, such as questions and instructions. Young people with receptive language difficulties may struggle to accurately follow instructions (particularly if they are multi-step), as such they may appear as if they are ignoring or defying the person giving the instructions. They may also repeatedly ask for clarification or repetition, by either turning to an adult or a peer.

Receptive language difficulties frequently co-occur with expressive language difficulties.

Retrieval Practice

This is a learning strategy where the focus is to get students to recall previously learnt information. For all learners, especially those who experience difficulties with their working memories, learning is not just about effectively storing information, it is also about their ability to access that information when it is required.

Retrieval practice techniques include regular, low-stake quizzes that test not only knowledge from the previous lesson but also knowledge that is going to be useful in the current lesson; spacing out of lessons (so that previously taught information can be revised); interleaving of lessons (where the teacher switches between topics – assisting the spacing of lessons) and feedback (so students can learn from their own mistakes).

S

Selective Mutism

Selective mutism is a severe anxiety disorder, where a person is unable to speak in certain situations e.g., at school or when around unfamiliar people. It is important to recognise that someone with selective mutism is not refusing to speak, they are unable to do so in particular situations. They may be able to speak freely around certain people, such as their family. It is more common in girls who speak English as a second language.

Contrary to popular belief, there is no connection between autism and selective mutism (although a person may have both). Also, mutism as a result of post-traumatic stress presents in a different way.

There are many therapies available to people with selective mutism, such as cognitive behaviour therapy. A person with this condition must not be pressured into speaking, as this is likely to have a negative impact. It is essential that if it is suspected that a child has selective mutism that they are referred to a speech and language therapist as soon as possible. The sooner a child is diagnosed and supported, the better.

Self-Injurious Behaviour

Self-injurious behaviour is a behaviour that causes physical harm to an individual. Children and young people with autism and learning difficulties may injure themselves for a number of reasons. It could start as a repetitive and soothing movement or a self-stimulatory behaviour, however it could develop into a way to attempt to communicate their needs or show they are distressed.

Self-injurious behaviours include head-banging, scratching or skin-picking, biting, poking (e.g., their ears, eyes or nose) and vomiting.

SEND Code of Practice (SEND CoP)

This is a statutory guide applicable to England. It contains details of legal requirements, which schools and colleges must adhere to without exception, as well as statutory guidance that must be followed by law, unless there is a good reason not to.

The SEND CoP details the duties of local authorities, schools and colleges, as well as health bodies, to provide for children and young people aged 0-25 years, with special educational needs.

It is often just referred to as the Code of Practice.

SEND Information Report

The SEND Code of Practice requires every school in England to publish a SEND Information Report, which must be made publicly available via their website.

The SEND Information report outlines the school's provision for learners with additional needs, it should also contain a link to the local authority's local offer. It explains how the school identifies, assesses and provides for students with SEND. It should also contain the name and contact details of the SENCO, as well as any other key members of staff.

The SEND Information Report should be reviewed and updated annually. It should also have the approval of the full governing body.

SEND Policy

The SEND Policy is a more detailed version of the SEND Information Report, it too must be publicly available on the school website and contain the name and contact details of the SENCO.

The SEND Policy goes into greater depth regarding the aims and objectives of the school for its learners with additional needs. It also explains how SEND are identified, how the graduated approach is applied, how students can leave the SEND register, how students and their families are supported, how those with medical needs are supported, how SEND provision is monitored and evaluated and what training and resources are available, among other key information.

The SEND Policy can be reviewed and updated every three years, as long as there is an up to date SEND Information Report available. Like most school policies, it needs to be ratified by the full governing body.

SEND Support – known as K

If a student is on the SEND register but does not have an EHCP, then they are said to be in receipt of SEND Support. This is recognised with the letter K on your school's management information system; those with an EHCP will be identified by the letter E.

Sensory and/or Physical Needs

This is one of the four broad areas of need – as outlined in the Code of Practice.

Some children and young people may have a vision impairment, a hearing impairment or a multi-sensory impairment and/or physical needs, which require additional long-term support and possibly specialist equipment. They may also experience sensory processing difficulties.

See Four Areas of Need and Sensory Processing Difficulties.

Sensory Discrimination Disorder

This is where a person struggles to understand what it is they have heard, seen, smelt, touched or tasted; for example being unsure whether someone has said 'mat' or 'map'.

They also experience difficulties with using their senses to learn or make judgements, for example they may forget how heavy something is, even if they have lifted it many times before.

Sensory Modulation Disorder

This is where a person is either over-responsive to sensory information, under-responsive or they are sensory craving.

Young people who are over-responsive appear hypersensitive to sensory information that most people would find tolerable – for example they may complain that the school bell is too loud, or the lights are too bright. For some young people they cannot articulate this hypersensitivity, so they demonstrate their feelings of discomfort through their behaviour, for example they may avoid certain situations or appear irritable.

Those who are under-responsive may appear withdrawn or in their own world. They may get into trouble at school for not responding to an adult's request. They may take a while to respond and could appear apathetic or disinterested.

Sensory seeking individuals may appear to always be 'on the go' They seek out new sensations and may enjoy things like messy play or climbing trees.

Sensory Processing Issues (or Disorder)

People with sensory processing issues may be more or less sensitive than others to what they see, hear, taste, touch or smell. Sensory processing issues can also affect balance and movement. Someone with sensory processing issues may exhibit inappropriate behavioural, motor, or adaptive responses after sensory stimulation. Triggers can include bright lights, loud noises or strong smells.

Some people with sensory processing issues will be sensory seeking, i.e., they may want to be hugged tightly, or they may like the feel of certain textures, such as soft materials or paint. At present there isn't a medical diagnosis for sensory processing issues.

Sensory processing issues commonly co-occur with autism and ADHD. There are three main categories of sensory processing issues.

See, Sensory Modulation Disorder, Sensory-based Motor Disorder and Sensory Discrimination Disorder.

Sensory-based Motor Disorder

Sensory based Motor Disorder is where an individual experiences difficulties with posture and/or planning and executing actions. People who struggle with their posture may move in a clumsy and disorganised manner, for example tripping up regularly.

See Dyspraxia.

Severe Learning Difficulties (SLD)

Children with severe learning difficulties are likely to find it difficult to understand, learn and apply new skills. Their cognitive difficulties may also co-exist alongside possible sensory, speech, language and communication needs. They may also experience physical difficulties and have social and emotional needs.

Learners with SLD will require a high level of support and should have an EHCP. They may attend mainstream schools or specialist provision.

Social Anxiety Disorder

A young person with social anxiety disorder has a persistent and intense fear of social situations. Everyday activities, such as going to the shops or school can trigger feelings of overwhelming anxiety. Early intervention is essential for supporting children with social anxiety disorder, as the more withdrawn they become the more challenging it is to encourage them to engage with education and social situations.

Social, Emotional and Mental Health Difficulties (SEMH)

One of the four broad areas of need – as outlined in the Code of Practice.

Learners with social and emotional needs may present in a variety of ways. They may be quiet and withdrawn; they may struggle to maintain positive relationships with their peers and/or they may behave in a way that disrupts their and other children's learning or has a negative impact on their health and wellbeing (e.g., self-injurious behaviour).

Mental health needs will be diagnosed by a healthcare professional (e.g., at CAMHS), they include anxiety, depression and eating disorders.

See Four Areas of Need.

Special Educational Needs and Disabilities Code of Practice

See SEND Code of Practice.

Special Educational Needs Coordinator (SENCO)

Every mainstream school must have a named SENCO. The SENCO is required to be a qualified teacher (i.e., has Qualified Teacher Status) and hold the NASENCO qualification (newly appointed SENCOs have three years in which to obtain this qualification).

Along with the headteacher and the governing body, the SENCO plays an important role in determining the strategic development of the school's SEND policy, as well as provision in the school.

SENCOs have the day-to-day responsibility for the coordination of provision for young people on the SEND register; they will provide guidance and training to colleagues; they work in collaboration with other professionals (such as educational psychologists and speech and language therapists) as well as parents/carers to ensure that the needs of everyone on the SEND register are being met.

Specific Language Impairment

See Developmental Language Disorder (DLD).

Specific Learning Difficulty (SpLD)

The term SpLD refers to a difficulty with specific aspects of learning. The most common examples of SpLDs are dyslexia, dyscalculia and dyspraxia (see individual definitions). They exist on a spectrum and although there are shared characteristics, each person is different and will have their own strengths and difficulties.

Speech and Language Therapist/Therapy (SALT/SLT)

Speech and language therapy provides treatment, support and care for people who have difficulties with communication (for physical or psychological reasons) or with eating, drinking and swallowing.

Speech and language therapists are allied health professionals who work with teachers, nurses, occupational therapists and doctors, as well individuals and their parents/carers.

Speech, Language and Communication Needs (SLCN)

SLCN is an umbrella term, used to describe difficulties impacting various aspects of language and speech. These include difficulties with receptive language, expressive language, pragmatic language, physical speech and fluency of speech.

SLCN difficulties are considered hidden disabilities, which can have long-term repercussions for a person's future outcomes, should they not get the required support.

People with a diagnosis of autism, ADHD, developmental language disorder and auditory processing disorder are recognised as having SLCN.

Spina Bifida

Spina bifida is when a baby's spine and spinal cord do not develop fully in the womb, causing a gap in the spine.

There are different types of spina bifida, with varying degrees of severity. Usually, when people refer to spina bifida they are referring to the most severe type: myelomeningocele. This is where the baby's spinal canal remains open along several vertebrae, allowing the spinal cord and protective membranes around it to push out and form a sac in the baby's back.

Most people with spina bifida have surgery to close the opening in the spine, however the nervous system will usually have already been damaged, which can lead to weakness or total paralysis of the legs, bowel and/or urinary incontinence, a loss of sensation in the legs and sometimes hydrocephalus.

Many young people with spina bifida have expected levels of intelligence, although some experience learning difficulties.

See Hydrocephalus.

Standardised Score

A standardised score converts an individual's raw score into one which compares it to their same-aged peers. This can be used to give an indication of how a student is performing relative to a sample of students of the same age. The average score is 100, so a score above this is considered above average, whereas a score below 100 is below average.

For students to receive certain additional support in examinations, the JCQ usually looks for a standardised score of below 85 (e.g., a student with a score of 84 in reading comprehension would be entitled to a reader). For some examination access arrangements, a student may require two scores below 70 – e.g., in an application for 50% additional time.

See Joint Council of Qualifications (JCQ) and Examination Access Arrangements.

T

Tangible Learning Aids

Tangibles are objects which can be held and manipulated in order to aid learning, they are sometimes referred to as manipulatives. They have been used as a learning tool for millennia; wooden blocks, counters and abaci are all considered to be tangible learning aids. Today we use similar objects, as well as more modern tangibles, including spellcheckers and Numicon (a mathematical aid from Oxford University Press).

Teaching Assistant (TA)

A TAs primary role is to support the learning of students in their care. TAs work with targeted students, who have identified additional learning needs, however usually they are employed to support all students, regardless of their needs. This may differ where a student has particularly complex needs and requires one to one or even two to one support (this is more likely to be the situation in specialist provision, rather than in mainstream settings).

It is the class teacher's duty to direct the TA in the lesson. Research over the past decade has found that it is less helpful for a TA to sit next to just one or two students for the entire lesson, as this can lead to learned helplessness and is not an effective way to support young people. Instead, it is better practice for a TA to circulate around the class, supporting a range of students. This also enables the class teacher to work one to one with any students with SEND who may require help - as they are the expert on their subject.

TAs work in settings throughout the key stages, although they may go by other names, such as Learning Support Assistant (LSA).

For further information, on the most effective way for teachers and TAs to collaborate and support learners, read Maximising the Impact of Teaching Assistants by Webster et al (see Useful Resources).

See Learned Helplessness.

Threat Perception

Some people are more sensitive to threat (whether real or perceived) compared to others. Individual differences towards threat perception are caused by a person's unique genetic inheritance as well as their personal experiences. Our threat perception ability develops and becomes more nuanced as we age.

Young people who have had adverse childhood experiences (e.g., an early childhood trauma of some description) are more likely to be 'hypervigilant' to any potential threats – seemingly aware of every sound, movement or smell; sometimes people confuse hypervigilance with the characteristic symptoms of ADHD, as the two can present similarly. For such children, something which may appear trivial could trigger a disproportionate emotional response.

See Adverse Childhood Experiences and Hypervigilance.

Tics

Tics are involuntary fast, repetitive muscle movements which result in sudden body jolts or sounds, they usually improve over time.

Examples of tics include blinking, grimacing, head jerking, finger clicking, coughing, sniffing or repeating a sound or phrase (occasionally this may be something offensive).

When tics last over a year, a person may be diagnosed with Tourette's syndrome. Sometimes tics can be a consequence of ADHD medications or neurological trauma.

See Tourette's Syndrome

Tourette's Syndrome

Tourette's Syndrome is a condition that causes a person to make involuntary sounds and movements called tics.

Tics can be physical (e.g., blinking, eye rolling or shoulder shrugging) and/or vocal (e.g., tongue clicking, whistling or throat clearing). In rare circumstances, individuals will swear but this affects approximately only one in ten people with a diagnosis of Tourette's.

Tics can worsen during times of stress or anxiety. People can learn to control their tics, although this does require a lot of concentration and energy, so they may experience a sudden release of tics when they can eventually relax.

Tics can lessen when a person is absorbed in an activity that requires a high level of concentration, for example, when playing a sport.

Tourette's is a neurodevelopmental condition and as such can co-occur with other neurodevelopmental conditions such as autism and ADHD.

See Tics and Neurodevelopmental Condition/Disorder.

Tribunal

The First-tier Tribunal or SEND Tribunal is an independent, national tribunal where parents and/or young people can appeal against a local authority's decision regarding special educational needs. It also hears claims of disability discrimination against schools.

For example, parents/carers and/or young people may appeal to the SEND Tribunal if they are dissatisfied with a decision regarding an EHC assessment or plan. There is no fee for them to pay. The local authority must comply with orders made by the SEND Tribunal.

The SEND Tribunal is governed by law and has to follow precedent (i.e., the interpretation of the law by higher courts in previous judgments about SEND disputes).

U

Umbrella Term

Umbrella Term is a phrase used to cover a number of different but related concepts. For example, Speech Language and Communication Needs (SLCN) and Neurodiversity are umbrella terms.

V

Velcro Effect

This describes support that is overbearing and offers few opportunities for a young person to make mistakes and to learn from them. It is often used in relation to teaching assistants who sit next to one student constantly and never leave their side.

See Learned Helplessness.

Vestibular

The vestibular system is our balance and movement sense, which tells us where our body is in relation to gravity, as well as the direction and speed at which we are travelling. Movement receptors are located in the inner ear and are essential for body posture, muscle tone and bilateral integration (the ability to use both sides of the body together in a coordinated way).

Children can experience difficulties as a result of either an overactive or under-responsive vestibular system; they may appear lazy or hyperactive, clumsy, inattentive, impulsive, or anxious.

Also see Sensory Processing Issues.

Visual Impairment (VI)

This is a term used to describe any kind of vision loss. A person can be registered as sight impaired (previously partially sighted) or severely sight impaired (previously blind).

Some children are visually impaired from birth, whereas others may experience vision loss after birth. Causes for vision loss include amblyopia (also known as a "lazy eye") and cataracts (sometimes caused by cancer treatments).

Visual Stress

See Meares-Irlen Syndrome.

Vocabulary Acquisition

This is the process of learning new words orally. For young people who have speech, language and communication needs, and/or those who are not exposed to talk early on in life, vocabulary acquisition can present as an area of difficulty.

Poor vocabulary acquisition has a significant impact on literacy skills, as there is a strong correlation between oral vocabulary and reading comprehension. After all, it is difficult to interpret what you are reading if you have no understanding of what the individual words mean.

Visit the Language and Reading Acquisition Lab website for further information. You will find a link in Useful Resources.

W

Working Memory

Working memory is a term used to describe a person's ability to hold and use new information, over a short period of time. It can be thought of as a mental workspace. Working memory is important when it comes to learning, for example, when solving multi-step mathematical problems, following instructions or remembering an unfamiliar word (e.g., in a modern foreign language lesson).

Difficulties with working memory capacity is at the root of many barriers to learning. Young people with speech, language and communication needs, or diagnoses such as dyslexia, dyscalculia or ADHD often experience difficulties with their working memory capacity. According to Gathercole and Alloway (2007), 70% of children with learning difficulties in reading score poorly on working memory assessments. Find a link to this 2007 paper by Gathercole and Alloway in Useful Resources.

See Phonological Working Memory.

X

Fragile X Syndrome (FRAX)

Fragile X Syndrome is the most common cause of an inherited learning disability. It can affect both sexes, although boys are usually more seriously affected as FRAX is caused by an alteration in the FRAX gene, which is part of the X chromosome. Learning difficulties can range from mild to severe.

Many people with FRAX display behaviours commonly associated with autism, such as difficulties with social interactions, struggling with changes to routine, avoiding eye contact and hand flapping. In fact, some individuals may receive a dual diagnosis of autism and FRAX.

Y

Young Person

In the SEND Code of Practice, a 'young person' is aged over 16 and under 25 years old.

In this book the term 'young person' is used interchangeably with 'child' and does not relate to a specific age group.

Z

Zone of Proximal Development (ZPD)

The ZPD is the difference between what a learner can do independently and what they can achieve with appropriate support.

This concept was developed by psychologist Vygotsky. He theorised that when a student is in the ZPD for a particular task, providing the right level of support will enable them to achieve success.

Support could be via a teacher or teaching assistant, a peer or through scaffolding (such as a writing frame or a key word list). The idea is that levels of support are reduced, as a learner becomes more competent and confident, until they can eventually complete the task unaided.

USEFUL RESOURCES

A hyperlinked and regularly updated version of the following resources can be found on the author's website: www.gemmacorby.com

Websites

Access Arrangements and Reasonable Adjustments (JCQ)

https://www.jcq.org.uk/wp-content/uploads/2020/08/AA-regs-2020-2021-version-for-website.pdf

ADHD Foundation

https://www.adhdfoundation.org.uk/

Dyslexic Fonts – Tes Article

https://www.tes.com/news/does-comic-sans-really-help-dyslexic-learners

Engagement Model – Guidance from the Standards and Testing Agency

https://www.gov.uk/government/publications/the-engagement-model

Helen Arkell Dyslexia Charity
https://www.helenarkell.org.uk/

Legal Advice
https://www.ipsea.org.uk or
https://www.senexpertsolicitors.co.uk/

Muscular Dystrophy (different types)
https://www.nhs.uk/conditions/muscular-dystrophy/types/

Maximising the Practice/Impact of Teaching Assistants
http://maximisingtas.co.uk/

NASEN
https://www.nasen.org.uk/

National Autistic Society
https://www.autism.org.uk/

Neurodiversity (Atlantic article by Harvey Blume)
https://www.theatlantic.com/magazine/archive/1998/09/neurodiversity/305909/

Reasonable Adjustments for Disabled Pupils (Equality Commission) https://www.equalityhumanrights.com/sites/default/files/reasonable_adjustments_for_disabled_pupils_1.pdf

Rose Report (full title: Identifying and Teaching Children and Young People with Dyslexia and Literacy Difficulties - 2009)

https://dera.ioe.ac.uk/14790/7/00659-2009DOM-EN_Redacted.pdf

SEND Code of Practice

https://assets.publishing.service.gov.uk/government/uploads/system/uploads/attachment_data/file/398815/SEND_Code_of_Practice_January_2015.pdf

Vocabulary Acquisition LARA

http://pc.rhul.ac.uk/sites/lara/

Working Memory (Gathercole and Alloway 2007 Paper)

https://www.mrc-cbu.cam.ac.uk/wp-content/uploads/2013/01/WM-classroom-guide.pdf

Books

Cowne et al (2015) The SENCO Handbook (Sixth Edition). Routledge: Abingdon

Webster et al (2015) Maximising the Impact of Teaching Assistants (Second Addition). Routledge: Abingdon

Printed in Great Britain
by Amazon